AUSTRALIAN ABORIGINES

Dr Richard Nile

Wayland

Titles in the series

Australian Aborigines
Bedouin
Inuit
Kurds
Maori
Native Americans
Rainforest Amerindians
Saami of Lapland
San of the Kalahari
Tibetans

Series editor: Paul Mason
Designer: Kudos Editorial and Design Services

Picture acknowledgements
The artwork on page 6 was provided by Peter Bull and that on page 19 was provided by Malcolm Walker.
The publishers would like to thank the following for allowing their photographs to be reproduced in this book: Mary Evans 35, 40; Eye Ubiquitous 4, 5, 7, 8, 10, 11, 12, 13, 14, 15, 16, 17, 18, 20, 22, 23, 24, 25, 26, 27, 29, 31, 32, 33, 34, 36, 37, 39, 41, 42, 43, 44, 45; Hutchison Photo Library 28; Paul Kenward 30, 38; Zefa 21.

First published in 1992 by
Wayland (Publishers) Ltd
61 Western Rd, Hove
East Sussex BN3 1JD, England

© Copyright 1992 Wayland (Publishers) Limited

British Library Cataloguing in Publication Data
Nile, Richard
    Australian Aborigines.- (Threatened Cultures Series)
    I. Title II. Series
    305.89

ISBN 0-7502-0371-4

Typeset by Malcolm Walker of Kudos Design
Printed and bound by Lego, Italy

Contents

Introduction

Australia is an ancient land. It is so old that once-giant mountains have been turned into small undulating hills by the weather. There were once great and lush forests in the interior; they have withered into deserts. The land is so old it is about as old as time itself. It may be the oldest land on earth.

Australia was probably once connected to South America, but the continents separated as the earth's plates moved. According to this theory the land mass that we now know as Australia drifted into what became the Indian and Pacific oceans. It is thought that the marsupials we now identify with Australia, such as kangaroos and wallabies, were once animals that lived in trees, like the marsupials of South America. As the continents separated, and Australia dried out and the centre became a treeless desert, so the tree creatures learnt to live on the ground.

Nobody knows for certain how or when the

Uluru is one of the best known of Australia's many natural landmarks and it is seen many Australian postcards and travel brochures. *Uluru* is also a place of tremendous cultural and spiritual significance for the *Aranda* peoples and other Aboriginal groups throughout Australia. For all Australians this largest of all known rock formations is the symbolic heart of the country.

This old man is one of the Pitjanjara people of central Australia. He is dressed in Western clothing but he knows many of the local Aboriginal languages and secrets.

Aborigines arrived in Australia. Nor does anybody know for certain where they came from. Perhaps they were always there.

At one time Australia may also have been connected to Asia by a giant land bridge. The Aborigines could have travelled down it from further to the north – possibly from the sub-continent of India. As ice ages came and went the land bridge dissolved into the ocean and those who had travelled down it would have been cut off from the rest of the world. Nobody knows for certain whether this is how it happened or not, but the oldest Aboriginal remains dated by modern scientists put the Aborigines at more than 60,000 years old. They have been in Australia for a very, very long time.

Many Aborigines do not agree that their ancestors were ever immigrants to Australia. Their own history tells them that they have lived there ever since Australia existed.

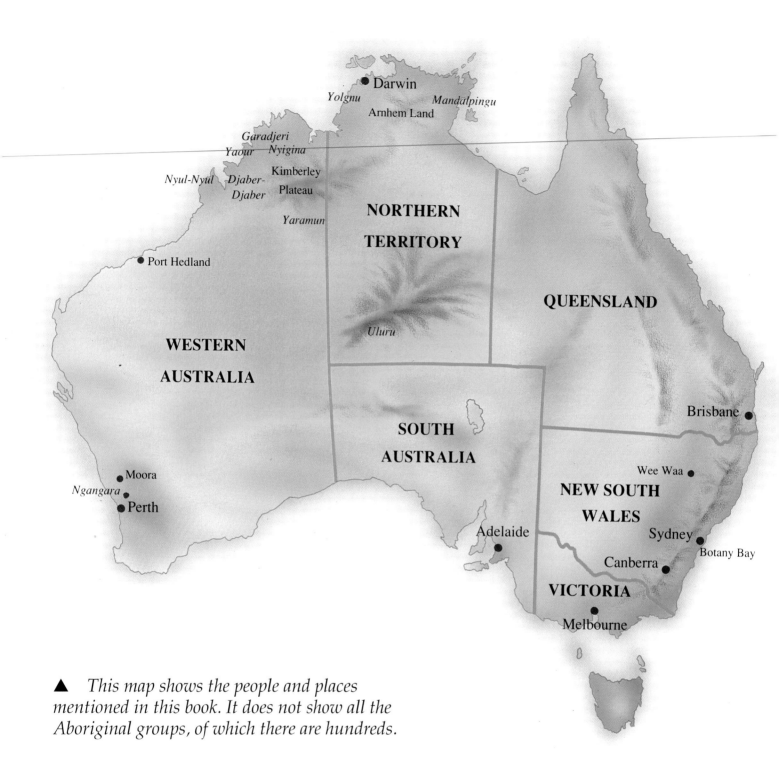

Darwin
Yolgnu
Mandalpingu
Arnhem Land

Garadjeri
Yaour Nyigina

Nyul-Nyul Djaber- Kimberley
Djaber Plateau

Yaramun

NORTHERN
TERRITORY

Port Hedland

WESTERN
AUSTRALIA

Uluru

QUEENSLAND

SOUTH
AUSTRALIA

Brisbane

Moora
Ngangara
Perth

Adelaide

Wee Waa

NEW SOUTH
WALES

Sydney
Botany Bay

Canberra

VICTORIA
Melbourne

▲   *This map shows the people and places mentioned in this book. It does not show all the Aboriginal groups, of which there are hundreds.*

Even if Australia was connected to South America or Asia, they say, and even if the ancient Aborigines did travel across land bridges, then they were not travelling into new lands. They were travelling in parts of the same land, because Australia was not a separate place. The Aborigines were not immigrants. They were the first people of Australia.

The Aborigines of Australia have a name for the time of creation. It is the Dreamtime. Then, the heavens and earth were one and the Ancestors were spirit men and women. The Dreamtime created heaven, earth and the people as three different parts of the same thing, that should never be divided. All traditional Aboriginal societies believed in the Dreamtime, and that because people were created from the land they could not survive without it.

2 The Aborigines

One of the first things that tourists notice about modern Australia when they go there is how few people actually live in such a big place. Most Australians live in one of the six major cities which are situated on the coast. Australia is about the same size as the USA (excluding Alaska), which has more than thirteen times as many people. It is an island-continent and the third largest country in the world. The distance between the east-coast city of Sydney and the west-coast city of Perth is the same as that between London and Moscow. Most of the country between is desert and sparsely populated.

Another thing tourists notice about Australia is that there are very few Aborigines among the crowds who live in the city. You can see people with origins in all parts of the world, but very few Aboriginal faces. There are some Aboriginal communities in the cities, but the others, who

▲   *The first settlement by non-Aborigines was made where Sydney now stands. The Aborigines who lived there were forced to move long ago, but today Aboriginal Australians are returning to Sydney in increasing numbers.*

started coming to Australia only 200 years ago, often did not like their presence. They have preferred that Aborigines live elsewhere. In consequence, most Aborigines tend to live on the fringes of cities and country towns or in outback communities. The other side of the coin is that many Aborigines prefer to live in rural environments, as the land is very important to Aboriginal culture.

TRACEY AND BUNDA

In the north-west of Western Australia, which is far removed from the cities, Tracey Nangala, an Aboriginal girl, lives with her family. She belongs to the *Yaramun* people of the Kimberley region, which is tropical on the coast and desert inland. She lives among her people in an all-*Yaramun* township. Tracey is taught the *Yaramun* ways and language but she also attends a school where she learns English, mathematics, social studies and all the things the non-Aborginal children learn in their schools.

On the other side of the Australian continent, Bunda Simms, who is around the same age as Tracey, attends the La Perouse primary school in Sydney and plays in the local junior Rugby

◀ *This girl is the product of two cultures. She shows all the outward signs of being influenced by non-Aboriginal culture but her identity is firmly Aboriginal. She lives in central Australia where her people still live traditional lifestyles.*

These boys celebrate Aboriginal identity with distinctive T-shirts. The flag is the Aboriginal flag. The red is said to be the colour of the ground and Aboriginal blood spilled over more than two hundred years. The gold is the sun and the black represents the Aborigines themselves.

League team. Bunda speaks English with what is known as the La Per Mob accent. Like Tracey, when he is at school he learns all the things other children learn, but unlike her he has not had the chance to learn any Aboriginal language.

Many people would say that Tracey lives a life as close as possible to being a traditional Aborigine, while Bunda lives very like the non-Aborigines. Certainly, they are both very different. Tracey's people still hunt and fish for their food and they cook in ways that have been practised for thousands of years. She knows the stories of her tribal ancestors as they are told to her by the elders and she will grow up knowing many of the secrets of her people.

Bunda, on the other hand, goes to the shops on Saturday mornings with his mum and dad to buy the family's food. He does not hunt and the only fishing he does is when he and a few friends ride their bikes down to Botany Bay –

▲ *Two hundred years ago the Aborigines could catch plenty of fish in Sydney Harbour. Now the water is so polluted that they are lucky to catch any at all.*

where white settlers first landed in 1788 – to toss their lines into the water. They do not catch many fish. The bay is so heavily polluted by large oil refineries and factories that not many fish survive in it. Bunda's family home is in the shadows of the large smoke stacks which now overlook Botany Bay.

Tracey Nangala lives in the wide open spaces of the north of Australia; Bunda Simms lives in a cramped corner of the city. At first sight they seem to have little in common with one another. Bunda would get lost in the *Yaramun* country and Tracey would feel quite overwhelmed by the city of Sydney. But they are similar in one

very important respect. They are both descendants of the first people to live in Australia, and like their forebears since the coming of the whites they have been treated unfairly and deprived of their rights and cultures by non-Aboriginal Australians.

Non-Aborigines sometimes make the mistake of saying that the only proper Aborigines today are those who live traditional lifestyles; that the only proper Aborigines are the 'full-bloods' and those who have not been influenced by non-Aboriginal ways. Most of these people have been killed off or have died out since 1788. But if you ask just about anyone from the *Yaramun* country or from the La Per Mob, they will soon set you straight. They will say, 'We are Aborigines alright', despite the wide differences between their lifestyles. They are Aborigines by descent and by inheritance.

When the *Yaramun* and the La Per Mob say they are Aborigines they are making a statement about their pasts and about their claims to be acknowledged as the first people of Australia. They are proud of their Aboriginal backgrounds, of their histories and cultures. No argument from non-Aboriginal points of view will make them want to be anything other than Aborigines. Their identity as Aborigines is fundamental to their whole way of life.

The mistake most often made by other people

This boy is wearing traditional face paint. People often think that the only real Aborigines are those who look like this. Do you think this boy would stop being an Aborigine if he took off the paint and put on jeans and a T-shirt? ▶

David Gulpilil is one of Australia's best-known actors. He was born in Arnhem Land in the north of Australia and he is a member of the *Mandalpingu* tribe. He was brought up to live a traditional Aboriginal life and has been initiated into the sacred customs of the *Mandalpingu*. Today he is the holder of many tribal secrets. He teaches young men how to hunt and fish, traditional secrets and ceremonies, and the meanings his people attach to the land and the many sacred sites on it. David Gulpilil is also a spokesperson for his people and he sits in council with other elders.

Like many present-day Aborigines David Gulpilil occupies two very different worlds. When David is making a film, or when he visits the cities, he trades his spears, his hunting sticks, *woomeras* and *boomerangs*, and his loin cloth for modern dress. In the cities he does all the things non-Aboriginal Australians do. He likes rap music, he goes to clubs, theatres and the movies, he visits the popular city beaches and their cafes and he drives his rented car along the freeways.

when talking about Aborigines is in their misuse of the word 'traditional'. When they say 'traditional Aboriginal cultures' they have in the back of their minds a world in which the Aboriginal way of life did not change for thousands of years. They have in mind a world that stood still until the coming of the white people. What they have failed to appreciate is that Aboriginal culture has always been changing. Changes in Aboriginal civilization were not the same as those of other civilizations. As far as we know Aborigines never developed a system of writing or complex machines. They probably remained hunters and gatherers rather

▼ *Wearing ceremonial body and face painting but in western clothing, these North-eastern Aboriginal women and men celebrate their Aboriginal identity at an annual festival at Townsville, a provincial city in the state of Queensland.*

▲   *In the 1950s Britain tested atomic bombs at Maralinga in South Australia. The area was not properly cleared and Aborigines born in the area still show signs of radiation poisoning. This artist has painted a picture using traditional dot patterns. It is overlaid with a picture of an atomic blast. Aboriginal groups from the Maralinga area are still trying to get the British government to clean up the area which looks like a wasteland.*

than developing agriculture or fixed settlements. But Aboriginal society has developed and changed to fit the Australian environment. The direction and pace of change has altered since the coming of the non-Aborigines.

THE REDFERN ABORIGINES

In the middle of Sydney, not far from the central railway station and close to where Bunda and his family live, a settlement of Aborigines has taken over the slums and turned them into an Aboriginal suburb. Here, the Redfern Aborigines run their own housing authority, their own schools, their own radio station, their own theatre groups and their own legal service. To many

Aboriginal art

To explain to children how parts of the land were made by different Ancestors (see page 39), Aborigines in the central regions of Australia often drew maps in the sand. These showed where the Ancestor came out, the footsteps he took while singing the land into existence, where he stopped to rest and where he went back in.

From these sand drawings there developed a style of Aboriginal art that has now become world famous. Galleries in Sydney, London, New York, Berlin and Paris pay large sums of money for Aboriginal art. This money can be used to fund co-operatives and educational schemes.

Aborigines the giant rock of *Uluru* in the centre of the continent is the spiritual heart of the country, while Redfern is the cultural and political heart of today's Aboriginal life. Redfern is the site where Aborigines have established their communities in defiance of intense pressure from some non-Aborigines not to do so. Redfern is a magnet for Aborigines from all over Australia when they travel to Sydney.

The community began modestly in the 1930s when Aboriginal workers and their families drifted into the city during the Depression in search of employment. Redfern was the cheapest, nastiest and most run-down part of the city. It was also a convenient drop-off point for those arriving in the city because it is so close to the railway station. Above all, it was about the only place in the city, apart from the segregated area of La Perouse just to the south of Redfern, in which Aborigines could live during a period when racial segregation was every bit as bad as apartheid in South Africa.

In the 1970s, Redfern also began to attract middle-class and intellectual Aborigines, because it was one of the few Aboriginal communities in the city. Among those who came to Redfern in the 1970s were poets, artists and politicians. Soon after completing a Harvard PhD, Roberta Sykes, who is a writer and campaigner for Aboriginal rights, moved to Redfern. Among her friends she counts the Aboriginal magistrate Pat O'Shane and the actor,

▲   *Children learn more about the richness of Aboriginal culture. The performance takes place in the front of a massive backdrop of traditional Aboriginal symbols including the Rainbow Serpent, which is an important source of life.*

▲ *A traditional sleeping shelter in northern Australia. Aborigines in Redfern have tried to make their houses have a similar 'open' feeling inside.*

Ernie Dingo, who featured in the second *Crocodile Dundee* film.

These people, among others, saw how the Aborigines could start to get other Australians to take account of their views. They saw the benefit of strength in numbers. Rather than choosing to move out of a poor part of the city as soon as they could, or simply never going there in the first place, they made their part of Sydney an exciting, interesting place for everyone who lived there. Soon, Redfern became the Australian centre of Aborigine cultural life. The radio station, the theatres, the schools and the legal centre all represent the success of Aboriginal culture all round Australia. The Aborigines established their community in the city's backyard and there they dug their heels in.

Redfern has improved the lives of the people who live there in many ways. Among the most important is the success of its housing policy. Redfern had been the slum area of central Sydney for as long as Sydney had been able to call itself a city. It was characterized by rows and rows of messy terraces and semi-detached houses. But the Aborigines who live in Redfern have adapted their housing to conform, within the confines of the city, with Aboriginal designs for dwelling. They call this indigenous inner-city architecture.

The Aboriginal settlement of Redfern from the 1970s onward happened at the same time as the city of Sydney itself began to change. Houses in old working-class areas were bought by wealthier people who liked the way they looked. The cost of housing increased so that many of the original inhabitants could no longer afford to live there.

The Aborigines resisted this development, and instead began to change the housing in Redfern to suit the needs of the Aborigines who lived in it. The terraces remained in place but the inside walls were knocked down. Whole interiors were rebuilt to suit the needs of extended families, which remain the basis of Aboriginal society. The houses were completely different from buildings non-Aborigines lived in, which were meant for smaller families.

The terraces were also painted in the red and white ochre of the western desert, with splashes of other colours to reflect contemporary Aboriginal culture. The new colour schemes and murals replaced the grimy brick faces of the slums, which were transformed into places with an Aboriginal identity. At the same time the narrow, enclosed verandas were turned into larger, communal areas. The few buildings that were knocked down made room for communal parks.

In Redfern schools, which are run according to the needs of the community, Aboriginal children begin by being taught Aboriginal languages, culture and history by Aboriginal teachers.

The residents of Redfern today can listen to Aboriginal programmes on the radio that play

▲ *Aboriginal students and parents demonstrate about the lack of Aboriginal Studies taught in Australian schools. Koori is another word for Aborigine.*

For years Australian musicians have experimented with a mix of Western and Aboriginal music. The most successful band of recent years is the all-Aboriginal group Yothu Yindi, who in 1991 were voted Australia's most popular band. Their hit single, Treaty, was voted the most popular Australian song for 1991.

music by Aboriginal performers, like the enormously popular *Yothu Yindi*, who were voted Australia's most popular band in December 1991. Their records are recorded in studios run by other Aborigines.

In Redfern there are also art studios and galleries featuring the work of Aboriginal artists like Tracy Moffit, who is also an acclaimed film-maker. There are dance and theatre groups too, all owned and run by Aborigines.

In Redfern today, traditional and modern Aboriginal cultures meet in a positive way. The past is remembered and treasured, but the community looks to the future. The terraces with their Aboriginal murals, designs and patterns, the legal service, the radio stations, the schools, the theatres, the art and recording studios are each giant symbols of optimism. They tell the story of the survival of peoples who not long ago seemed likely to die out.

Police brutality

In Redfern, as everywhere else, Aborigines have been treated brutally by the police. In a recent incident, an innocent man was shot dead in his bed when police broke in, looking for someone else, they said. The dead man's wife saw her husband being shot. Their children were woken up by the noise, and rushed in to see their father lying dead in a pool of blood. Nobody was ever charged with the murder and no apology was ever offered by the police.

▲ *A mass demonstration of 20,000 Aborigines in 1988, protesting against the high level of prejudice against Aborigines in Australia.*

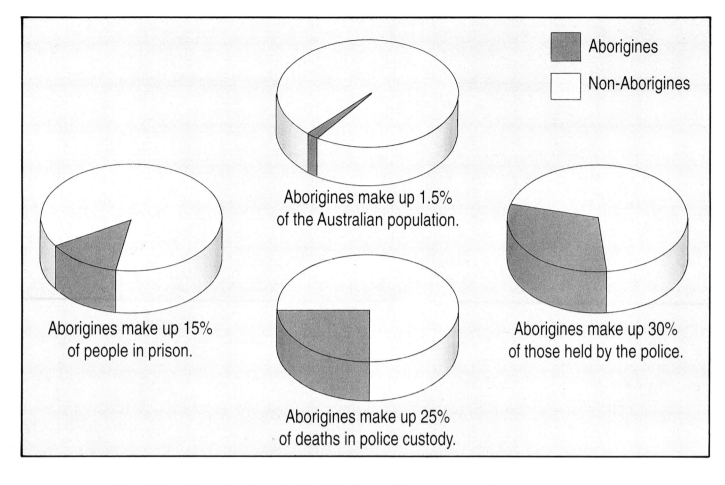

Aborigines make up 1.5% of the Australian population.

Aborigines make up 15% of people in prison.

Aborigines make up 25% of deaths in police custody.

Aborigines make up 30% of those held by the police.

Aborigines

Non-Aborigines

▲ *Many Aborigines have had to deal with the police at some time.*

One alarming trend from 1980-1990 was an increase in the number of deaths of Aborigines in prisons or in police custody. Many more people die in detention than is commonly known. Some inmates die naturally and others die as a result of accidents. There are also some who commit suicide or die violently by someone else's hand. Aboriginal deaths in custody are occurring at an alarmingly high rate in Australia.

Aborigines represent approximately 1.5 per cent of the population of Australia but they make up 15 per cent of the prison population. This means that if you are an Aborigine and you live in Australia, you are ten times more likely to be imprisoned than if you are a non-Aborigine. Aborigines also make up about 30 per cent of all people held in police detention, so if you are an Aborigine in Australia you are twenty times more likely than a non-Aboriginal person to be

arrested and placed in the lock-up. Finally, although Aborigines only make up 1.5 per cent of the Australian population they make up almost a quarter of all deaths in custody.

Very few Aborigines pass through their lives without coming into direct contact with the police and courts. Most have experienced jail life or have brothers, sisters, cousins, friends, mothers, fathers, sons and daughters who have been in jail at one time or another.

There are many explanations for the high rate of detention. Firstly there is the racism of the police forces, who for many years have discriminated against Aborigines without having to answer for it to any higher authority. For the police, the Aborigines have been easy picking. The courts may not have been as biased against Aborigines as the police, but they have generally believed the police's version of events. This has

▲   *Relations between the police and Aborigines have never been very good and Aborigines have often been victims of police brutality. Today, police are being trained not to discriminate but there is still a long way to go before prejudice is broken down.*

happened even in cases where independent witnesses have testified against methods of arrest, and where police have used excessive force. More than one court has heard witnesses tell how innocent Aborigines have been wrongly arrested, but until recently this has made little difference and Aborigines have been wrongly convicted. In many areas Aborigines have either inadequate legal representation or none at all. When they do have proper legal help, the conviction rate drops. The Aboriginal Legal Service, in which Aboriginal and non-Aboriginal lawyers work together, is helping to make sure that increasing numbers of Aborigines are legally represented.

The problem is made worse by the generally low social and economic position which the Aborigines occupy in Australia. Despite the successes of Redfern and similar communites elsewhere in Australia, many Aborigines live in a more or less constant state of poverty and homelessness. Some of them could only provide themselves with a reasonable standard of living by stealing. They also come into conflict with non-Aborigines whose standard of living is much higher than their own. The Aborigines always come off second best.

Some Aborigines see crime as a means of relieving boredom. Among teenagers in particular, where younger teenagers stay away from school and older teenagers are often unemployed, joy-riding in stolen high-powered cars has become a dangerous way of finding something different to do. Alcohol and drug taking are also reactions to poverty, and are closely linked to crime. Alcohol and drugs make a lethal cocktail in a stolen car and many people have been killed and injured.

When non-Aboriginal people have been killed in the recklessness, anger against Aborigines has intensified. In 1992 in Western Australia very harsh penalties were introduced to try to

▲ *Aborigines on the old reserve at Hermannsburg in central Australia. The reserve system has now been abandoned because it was so inhumane; people were forced to live in crowded conditions in inadequate shelter with no proper washing facilities or toilets.*

stop joy-riding. These penalties are not really any solution; the causes of the boredom that leads to joy-riding are poverty and dissatisfaction with the place Aborigines are forced to take in Australian society. It is hard to see how long prison sentences will help.

During the last decade, Aborigines have died in custody in Australia at the rate of one every two weeks. A recent national inquiry into Aboriginal deaths in custody found three main causes of death: suicide, violence and natural causes. Among those cases dealt with was the death in 1981 of Eddie Murray. Aged twenty-one when he died, Eddie Murray was from Wee Waa in New South Wales. He was arrested for drunkenness, and later found hanged in his police cell. At the time, Eddie, who had been a champion footballer, was the only prisoner in the cell. His cell had been locked with a key that only the police had access to. The coroner found that he had been killed 'at the hands of a person or people unknown.' To this day, nobody has been arrested for the murder of Eddie Murray.

Every police force in Australia has similar

▲   *Aboriginal demonstrators protesting against the rate of detention of Aborigines in Australian jails. The picture of the man's face on the far left is that of Eddie Murray who was killed in a police cell in 1981.*

▲ *People are still angry and afraid about Aboriginal deaths in custody, despite a commission of inquiry which handed down its judgement in 1991.*

suspicious cases of deaths in custody recorded. The commission of inquiry was begun after the death of a sixteen-year-old, John Pat, who died in his prison cell after being arrested in Port Hedland in Western Australia. Several people saw five policeman repeatedly kick John Pat in the upper region of his body after he had been knocked to the ground during a disturbance. He died of a brain haemorrhage in his police cell a few hours after the incident. The police officers denied that they had kicked John Pat and claimed that they had used no more force than they normally would while arresting someone. A separate investigation was held but, as with the murder of Eddie Murray, no one was ever charged. The list of deaths and suspicious circumstances continues, and even now justice is often not done.

The commission of inquiry, which handed down its findings in 1991, noted that suicide rates were high among Aboriginal prisoners, particularly young Aboriginal men who were confined to small cells. Many hanged themselves using shoe laces, football socks, belts or blankets.

The reason for the high occurrence of suicide is not known. Alcohol and drugs are sometimes blamed, especially when they led to depression or hallucinations. A commonly-held theory is that, terrified by isolation and confined areas, Aborigines under the influence of drugs or alcohol believe they are being possessed by evil spirits. But more generally, for people so used to space, confinement is horrific.

Most people agree that too many Aborigines end up in Australian jails and that strong action should be taken to stop the deaths in custody. In 1992 a TV programme, featuring an amateur video taken in secret, showed police officers making fun of Aborigines who died in custody, revealing racist attitudes in police forces. It is plain that Aborigines are easy targets for the police, and retraining programmes have now begun for police officers, to try to break down their prejudices.

Education

Australia is a lucky country and it has one of the highest standards of living in the world. It is a society where most people would claim that there are equal opportunities for everyone. But of all the ethnic groups that live in Australia the Aborigines are socially and culturally the most disadvantaged. They occupy the lowest position in just about every aspect of society as measured by health, living conditions, education and employment. They live, on average, twenty years less than non-Aboriginal Australians. Infant mortality is shockingly high in comparison with non-Aboriginal groups. The conditions under which the majority of Aborigines live

▲   *Increasingly, non-Aboriginal Australians are questioning Australia's black history. Here two demonstrators draw attention to the low life-expectancy and shocking level of infant mortality among Aborigines.*

resemble in many ways those of the world's poorest countries, rather than those of one of the world's richest. Part of the reason for this is the years of neglect on behalf of non-Aboriginal policy makers. Apart from training Aborigines to a low level where they could read and write (though many are still illiterate), until quite recently teachers were not trained to cope with the special needs of Aboriginal children. Most teachers seemed to be quite uninterested in passing on to Aborigines the benefits which an education so obviously brings.

As a result of their own efforts, and with some help from the government, opportunities for Aborigines to become doctors, lawyers and headteachers have increased. But Aboriginal children are even now likely to leave school at an early age, and comparatively few make it into universities or other institutions of higher education.

Recently teachers have looked into the ways the education system has treated Aboriginal children, and most agree that the ways schools have normally run in Australia have not

▲ *These Aboriginal children in Redfern were among the leaders of a school strike there, protesting about the lack of Aboriginal Studies in the classroom.*

▲ *In remote outback areas children may not have learnt English until they went to school, which put them at a great disadvantage in all their classes, which were taught in English.*

addressed the special needs of Aboriginal students. One of the key problems is that for many Aborigines English is a second language, but it is taught in schools as a first language. So when teachers speak to Aboriginal students they do not take account of the fact that many are used to speaking a different language. Imagine going to school and finding that your teacher expected you to understand a lesson in Spanish. He or she would probably think you were stupid, just as many non-Aboriginal teachers have thought Aboriginal children were stupid because they found it hard to understand English.

This language problem is most obvious in areas in the outback where traditional languages are still spoken. But even in the cities and the country towns where many of the old ways have been lost, the Aborigines speak what language specialists call creole. This is a combination of English and the Aboriginal language.

The fact that many Aboriginal children are more familiar with their traditional language than English has only now been taken into account. Aborigines are no more or less intelligent than their non-Aboriginal counterparts. The two peoples simply looked at

▲ *Some attempt has been made at this school at the Stirling Station to make the heat bearable. Still, the children would prefer to be taught outside where it is cooler.*

things in different ways and thought about these things using different languages. The school system favoured English, not the language of the Aboriginal children. Not surprisingly, the Aboriginal children tended to fall behind.

Most Aboriginal children have been educated under this system and have suffered as a consequence. As they became identified as having learning difficulties, any hopes they might once have had of success at school disappeared. Teachers began to expect Aborigines to fail, and Aboriginal students were put at the bottom of the class even before the first tests were taken. It was assumed that they

would perform badly. This meant that even those who had good English language skills and who were capable of advancing under the system suffered unfairly. There was very little in the Australian education system for Aborigines. It merely confirmed their low status in society and reinforced in non-Aboriginal people the view that Aborigines were inferior.

Educators are now trying to improve the situation, but they have to try and change the practices and perceptions of more than 200 years. It is likely to take several generations of teachers and students, both Aboriginal and not, to change the situation. But the change has started and special language training for teachers and Aboriginal students has begun in Australian schools. There are even a few schools which specialize in Aboriginal languages. At these English is taught as a second language rather than as a first, in the same way as you might learn French at school.

In Western Australia, Aboriginal elder Mr Ken Colbung has started an all-Aboriginal school called *Ngangara*, where the students learn first about their own customs and cultures and then apply what they learn to their other subjects. They learn about their own identity as Aborigines first and then they do maths, social studies, English and all the other things non-Aboriginal children learn at school. The school is proving a great success and Aboriginal children are leaving it with a better chance of succeeding in the outside world than other Aborigines who attend non-specialist schools.

The Aboriginal students who are now graduating from specialist schools are no different in terms of their academic achievements than their non-Abriginal counterparts in other schools. There is a lot of pressure on these students to succeed educationally and return to the school system, where they will take on the responsibilities of teaching a new generation of Aboriginal students. Until very recently, Aboriginal teachers were completely unknown.

◀ *Paul Coe first became well-known as a campaigner for Aboriginal rights in 1988. Here he speaks out about racism in Australian schools.*

Survival

Not far north of *Ngangara*, near the township of Moora which is about 200 km north of Perth, there used to be an Aboriginal reserve. It was closed down in the early 1980s but before that it had been the home of hundreds of people. Not far away Benedictine monks and Methodist preachers had established missions, where they kept Aboriginal children who had been taken away from their parents. Less than a generation ago it was common practice to take Aboriginal babies from their mothers and put them into institutions where they grew up without parents. Even today there are disputes over the custody of Aboriginal children.

The Aboriginal reserve was located 3 km out of Moora. The houses were not suitable for

◀ *These children live on the Mossman Mission. In the past missionaries took children away from their parents and put them into institutions, where they grew up alone.*

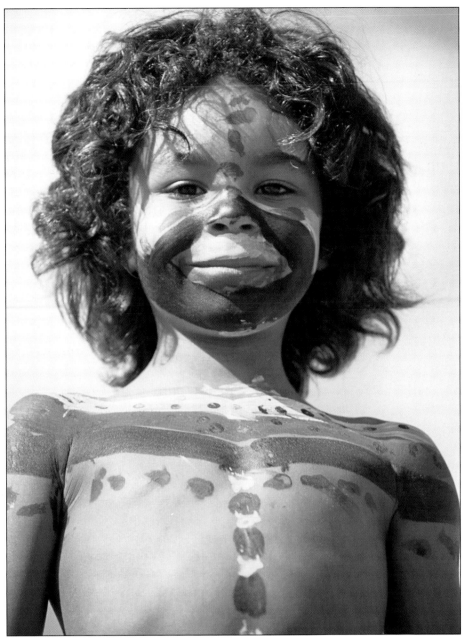

An Aboriginal boy with modern-style face and body painting. The design is a development from the face and body painting of traditional society.

people to live in. Most were one- or two-bedroom huts made out of corrugated iron. There was no insulation to keep out the great heat in summer or to keep the buildings warm in winter. There was no electricity or running water, and one toilet block served the needs of the entire makeshift community of five hundred people, in which as many as five families shared a single hut.

The reserves created massive social problems throughout Australia, and the overcrowding and the insanitary conditions meant that infectious diseases soon spread. The children and the old people suffered most, especially in the winter. Colds and flu soon developed into pneumonia, from which many died. The houses were cold and the roofs leaked. Once the damp got into clothing and blankets it was virtually impossible to dry them out. The clothes people wore, often given to them by charities, were no barrier to the cold and wet. The reserve system had to come to an end because it was so inhumane. The reserves were eventually closed down, but not before a great deal of damage had been done.

▲ *Aboriginal men in traditional face and body paint perform a traditional dance. Many dances have symbolic significance; usually they imitate the movements of animals.*

Given that the Aborigines have been so badly treated in the past and that non-Aboriginal Australians have done their best to break down the structures of Aboriginal society, it is amazing that there are any Aborigines still living in Australia. It is true that many of the traditional ways of the Aborigines have been layered over by non-Aboriginal ways, but these days Aborigines are proudly saying that they are both Aborigines and Australians. In doing so they are finding out more and more about their history and traditions. This is refreshing for many who were used to hearing themselves talked about in the terms that non-Aboriginal people used; hopeless, layabout, lazy and drunkard.

Paddy Roe was born around the turn of the century in the *Nyigina* tribe of the Kimberley region of Australia. Today he keeps tribal secrets for the *Nyigina* and for other tribes of the area, including the *Garadjeri*, *Yaour*, *Nyul-Nyul* and *Djaber-Djaber*. He calls his homeland *Gularbulu*, which means the coast where the sun goes down. His tribal lands are made up of sandy beaches, undulating coastal foothills and mangrove swamps.

When he was a child, the police tried to take Paddy Roe away from his parents and place him in an institution, but he was saved when he was hidden away under a blanket while the authorities searched the camp site. Each time the authorities came back he was hidden away. It is good that Paddy escaped, because he became initiated as a full member of the *Nyigina* and later became the keeper of its tribal secrets. Paddy Roe is now able to pass on to succeeding generations the secrets of his tribal history. If he had been captured and raised in an institution, these secrets would have been lost forever. The young people of the *Nyigina* are are fortunate to be able to know about their past.

Paddy Roe is one of only a few tribal elders initiated into tribal secrets. For other tribes, especially those who have lived where non-Aboriginal settlements now flourish, almost all the tribal ways have been lost.

Nearly 1,700 km to the south of *Nyigina* territory is the city of Perth on the west coast. There, Sally Morgan grew up in a mixed-blood family. But she grew up not knowing her Aboriginal background. Her friends at school knew that she had dark skin but her mother told her that she was Indian. At school, Sally was

◀ *Body marking and ceremonial dress are an important part of traditional life for the Aborigines. This old man has a sharp bone, possibly taken from an emu, piercing his nose.*

treated as quaint, exotic and beautiful. Had it been known that she was an Aborigine, she would have been treated as inferior. Sally was always troubled by the story of her Indian past, and she could not understand why, whenever she had visitors, her grandmother would retreat into her room and refuse to be seen by anyone. Sally later learned that her grandmother was hiding the fact that she was an Aborigine. Sally could pass for an Indian at school and not many people seemed to identify her mother as an Aborigine, but her grandmother was obviously an Aborigine.

Sally eventually discovered that she was not an Indian whose parents had migrated to Australia but an Aborigine. At first she was shocked – surely she really was an Indian beauty, not one of those Aborigines? But it was true, as her mother and grandmother told her. Sally's mother had spent much of her childhood in non-Aboriginal institutions; her grandmother had worked as a domestic servant for white cattle barons. Sally decided to find out more about her people and her own identity, which had been hidden away from her.

Sally's decision to find out about her background started her on a path that led to the discovery of a culture that would otherwise have been completely lost to her. She began by asking questions of her mother and grandmother. Eventually, she visited the birthplace of her grandmother in the north of Australia. There she met relatives she did not know she had. She found out more and more about her own history

▲ *An Aboriginal mother, and daughter. In the past, children from mixed-race marriages have hidden their Aboriginal background, or never been told about it, to avoid discrimination.*

▲   *This old photograph shows a man being painted. It also reveals some of the ways in which traditional Aborigines used Western implements and adapted them to their own lifestyles, such as the blankets covering the humpy (temporary home).*

and the history of her people.

Sally learned from her mother and grandmother about the cruelty that they had suffered at the hands of the non-Aborigines. She came to understand why her family had hidden the fact that she was an Aborigine. It was because she had a better chance at life in Australia if she was not thought of as an Aborigine. The decision was taken by the family so that Sally did not suffer in the way that her mother and grandmother had. Discovering that she was an Aborigine and learning about her family's tragedies made Sally determined to tell the world what had happened. She was determined to show everyone that she was an Aborigine, instead of hiding the fact.

Sally Morgan's discovery of her true identity resulted in a moving book called *My Place*, which became a bestseller in Australia and won

many literary awards. In it Sally Morgan tells her own story. Today Sally Morgan lives in Perth where she works as a writer, artist and activist on behalf of Aboriginal causes in Australia. In the north of the state Paddy Roe passes on traditional stories to younger generations of Aboriginal children.

The negative images of Aborigines are being turned around. Slowly, non-Aborigines are also beginning to learn more and more about their prejudices and the things that they have done to the Aborigines. Through people like Paddy Roe and Sally Morgan, a more positive image of Aborigines is being presented. Both Aboriginal and non-Aboriginal Australians are discovering what it really means to be an Aborigine. Not that you are a lazy, drunken, stupid and useless person, but that you have a proud past that goes back to the time when Australia first existed.

▲   *These painted markings on rocks signify a place of importance for Aborigines in the Katherine Gorge in northern central Australia.*

According to Aboriginal myths, religions and beliefs, the land is the source of all life and meaning. The land and the lives of the people are intimately bound up with one another. Everything is connected with everything else and all has a spiritual significance. The land, the people, the flora and fauna, were all created during the Dreamtime.

The Dreamtime is the single most powerful and important myth in the Aboriginal belief system. It is the story of how the world was made and is very significant to Aborigines. The Dreamtime exists beyond normal time and way beyond the collective memories, stories and knowledge of even the wisest elders. It is a sacred time; a time of great cosmic forces when the spiritual, physical and moral worlds were in the making. The whole Aboriginal universe dates itself back to this vague but powerful distant past.

Aborigines believe that in death they will be reunited with their ancestors. They also believe that the Dreamtime will come again and give new life to traditional Aboriginal values and customs. This is a powerful myth that has been retold many times in terms of present-day dissatisfaction, as a way of encouraging Aborigines to believe in a positive future. The Dreamtime is also a rallying political symbol, since it will result in a cleansing of the earth and the return of lands to the Aborigines.

The Aborigines are a deeply religious people, but there are no priests in Aboriginal society, as there are in most other religious societies. Instead there are elders who translate the messages of the spirit world and pass these on to other tribal members. These special men and women have special responsibilities and powers within Aboriginal communities. They are especially responsible for the young people.

Traditional Aboriginal society is filled with rituals which relate to the spirit world. The spirits live in the earth and in the sky. They are everywhere and they give significance and meaning to the environment. A spirit can inhabit a desert flower, a tree or a bush; it can give shape to hills, plains and rocks; it can be seen at work in the habits of humans and animals. According to Aboriginal religion, the physical and spiritual worlds are one and the same thing. The earth is the mother of all things. If one is upset, the other will be as well.

Traditional Aboriginal societies have many ritual ceremonies. One of them is the *Corroborree*. A *Corroborree* is a ceremonial event which traditionally marks an important

▲   *This rock formation in northern Australia, the 'Devil's Marbles', has been deemed a place of evil spirits by the local Aborgines.*

occasion in society. It is a festival of spirits. *Corroborrees* are normally held at night. They involve a good deal of music, dancing and other rituals. Men and women are painted in sacred patterns with different coloured paints. These are made by grinding down rocks and mixing the powder with water, and oil from the emu. People also wear feathers and animal skins.

In traditional Aboriginal society, men and women have their own rituals, stories and ceremonies, as well as the ones like *Corroborrees* that they all attend. At a *Corroborree*, the men play *didgeridoos*, which are long straight wind instruments made by hollowing out the branches of trees. The sound of the *didgeridoo* is haunting and quite unlike any other instrument. Its deep growling noises combine with high squealing pitches that penetrate the night. In dance the men and the women recreate the characters of different animals. The men click their sticks, their *boomerangs* and their *woomeras* to keep the rhythm. People also sing when they are not dancing. Everyone sits in a large circle around the night-time fire.

Today traditional *Corroborrees* are held in secret for those initiated into the ways of ancient Aborigine customs. But comparatively few contemporary Aborigines know the ways of their ancient forebears, so they do not *Corroborree* exactly as the ancient Aborigines

▲   *The* didgeridoo *is a traditional Aboriginal instrument, played at ceremonial events such as* corroborree. *Here, it is being used as part of a performance of traditional dancing.*

did. But they do observe features of ancient ritual and many of the dances that have become popular art forms with contemporary Aborigines can be traced back to the old dances.

Rituals, religion and Aboriginal customs are all means by which traditional society maintains links between past, present and future. Beliefs are passed down by word of mouth to each successive generation. *Corroborrees*, dance, music and stories all relate to the physical and moral world. This spiritual attachment to place also means that Aborigines do not believe in the concept of personal property. As nomadic peoples, they traditionally held that the abundance of the earth belonged to all that travelled on it. In present-day society they believe in equality and sharing.

Just over 200 years ago, something interrupted Aboriginal ways, and changed the land and Aboriginal lifestyles forever.

▲ *These paintings at Kakadu National Park in the Northern Territory are thousands of years old. They are periodically repainted so that they do not fade.*

How the world was made

Aboriginal beliefs hold that in the Dreamtime, the Ancestors came up from under the earth and walked over it, singing. What they sang was created as they walked. Their singing created the world, and they walked and sang until they were tired, and then they went 'back in'. The places where each Ancestor went back under the earth are important religious sites, linked by the steps the Ancestor took on his journey and the places he stopped to rest. These sites can be rocks, pools, hills and many other parts of the landscape.

Bodysnatchers

During the nineteenth century, museums all round the world wanted to have the skeletons of different people from all round the world to keep in their collections, and they would pay a lot of money for them. Non-Aborigines, mostly Europeans, began stealing the corpses of dead Aborigines to sell their skeletons. As if this was not disgusting enough, when they could not find Aborigines who had already died they began murdering them.

Despite the fact that the skeletons were stolen and never had funeral ceremonies, many museums around the world still refuse to return them to their families.

In 1788, the Europeans arrived with the intention of making permanent settlements in Australia. How bewildering and shocking these new people must have seemed to the Aborigines, who had never seen anything like the pale-skinned people before. At first they thought the newcomers were the spirits of ancient ancestors, for all ghosts are white, and that a new Dreamtime had begun. But this Dreamtime soon turned into a nightmare. Soon the Aborigines found out what the white settlers were really like. After this time things could never be the same again.

From thriving communities which lived in harmony with one another and with the earth, the Aborigines became a group of people threatened with destruction.

When the first white settlers arrived in Australia in 1788, they immediately occupied Aboriginal land and began killing the fish and animals the Aborigines depended on. In 1789 a smallpox epidemic killed almost half the Aborigines living near Botany Bay. The Aborigines fought a guerrilla war against the whites, but were no match for their guns and horses.

The settlers could not understand that the Aborigines claimed land they did not physically occupy all the time as their own, and assumed that they could simply take it. When the Aborigines resisted, the settlers shot them. During the nineteenth and early twentieth century, many Aboriginal groups from coastal and eastern Australia were destroyed. The groups that survived were mostly those that lived in the interior, where the land was too barren for the settlers.

Just over 200 years ago, the Aborigines made up 100 per cent of the population of Australia. Today they make up 1.5 per cent of the population. There may have been as many as three million Aborigines in 1788; nobody knows for certain. They now number about 250,000, although this number is increasing all the time. Two hundred years ago there were more than 250 Aboriginal languages. Today, traces of fewer than half that number survive.

In their own country Aborigines have been considered outsiders. They have been forced from many of their traditional lands, and not allowed to follow their traditional ways of life. Today, the Aborigines are fighting back and bit by bit they are beginning to win recognition of their civilization, which was so violently affected by the coming of the Europeans.

Sadly, changes have come too late for some

people. The more positive and confident assertions of Aboriginal identity cannot help those who have died in police custody. They can only slowly begin to prevent the alcoholism and drug addiction that are so common in Aboriginal communities. They can only slowly improve the conditions under which most Aborigines live, and which most non-Aborigines accept as normal.

Australia's present-day population of almost eighteen million is made up of people from many different societies, cultures and countries. They have all made new homes in Australia, which now hosts one of the most diverse collections of peoples anywhere in the world.

The non-Aboriginal population, which can trace its origins back to Asia, Africa and the Americas, and most commonly Europe, lives side by side, mostly happily. The non-Aborigines are rightly proud of this achievement. Few societies with so many differences have achieved the same degree of social harmony.

Yet Australia's original inhabitants remain socially and culturally disadvantaged and subject to terrible racism. Where the non-Aborigines have tried to end racism among one another, they continue to practise it on the Aborigines.

The *Yolgnu* people of Arnhem Land in the north of Australia have a special term which means the resolution of conflict. It is *Makarrata*.

▲ *A way in which Aboriginal communities have sought to stop the devastation of their people by alcohol and drug abuse is to create alcohol-free areas called grog free zones.*

Friendships and political alliances cross racial boundaries. Jo Valentine is an Australian Senator for the Nuclear Disarmament Party. She is embraced by Aboriginal writer and activist Faith Bandler.

In traditional society *Makarrata* was usually reached only after lengthy discussions between the elders of the tribe. These discussions were held at *Corroborrees*.

For the *Yolgnu*, *Makarrata* implies peaceful co-existence and harmony between peoples. Its meaning has now been expanded so that many Aborigines think about *Makarrata* in their dealings with non-Aboriginal Australians.

The Aborigines want to be able to negotiate with non-Aboriginal Australians on an equal footing, but many non-Aborigines remain suspicious of them. They say the Aborigines want to form a political structure like a parliament which has similar authority to the Australian parliament. They feel that such a body would mean that the Aborigines wanted to separate from the rest of the country. But the Aborigines and some non-Aborigines argue that for *Makarrata* to work there must be full and equal discussion between both parties. Otherwise, the Aborigines are in an inferior position. The Aborigines have already had 200 years of being

in an unequal position. Now they want an equal voice. They want an Aboriginal council through which they can negotiate with the immigrants to their country.

The Aborigines have been forced by non-Aborigines to give up much that was once central to their society and culture. They have lost their lands, many of their languages and whole systems of belief. But they have not lost their identity as the first inhabitants of Australia. They now want to make sure that they are no longer treated as though they do not belong in their own country.

Most importantly, the Aborigines are calling for a *Makarrata* over questions of land. They want their claims to the land to be recognized by the non-Aboriginal law makers. Ultimately, this involves a fuller recognition of the Aborigine's rights to their own culture, which have been denied for so long. The land is sacred to the Aborigines of Australia and according to the Dreamtime myth, it is the source of all life. Even for contemporary Aborigines, living in the hearts of cities, the land is like one continuous and massive place of worship. It is the spiritual base of the people. It is their home and the place of their well-being. Without the land the Aborigines feel they are separated from their life source, that they are separated from their spirit.

Today Aborigines are claiming a right to the land, not only for religious reasons but also to allow their culture to once again flourish. With land, some would be able to continue their traditional hunting and gathering of food. Others could run their own cattle or livestock stations. But, in asking for land to be returned, the Aborigines are not asking for property rights in the way that non-Aboriginal Australian society understands property. For them the land can belong to no individual. The Aborigines want to bring the culture and the land back into harmony and thereby reassert their Aboriginal identity.

Non-Aboriginal Australia has never formally acknowledged that the Aborigines are the original people of the land. In recent years Aborigines have begun to agitate to have part of their lands returned and to get some formal acknowledgement that the land is theirs – that the land was taken illegally. They want a treaty which gives full recognition of their claims. Such a treaty would also help other people to understand their claims for Aboriginal culture as a whole.

▲   *The 1988 Bicentenary celebrations brought about both protests and friendships. Here a group of people demonstrate under a flag that says, 'We all walk on Aboriginal land'.*

The future

On Australia Day, 26 January 1988, non-Aboriginal Australia was in a mood for a party. The day marked 200 years since the first white people had come to live in Australia. Out of very little these people had built one of the most successful societies in the world. Their forebears had overcome some of the most difficult territory in the world and come together over enormous distances to form a single nation. All around people could see what had been accomplished over two centuries.

On the very same day the largest gathering of Aborigines since the Dreamtime took place at the site where the white celebrations were happening. More than 20,000 Aborigines from all parts of Australia assembled first at Redfern and then marched down to Sydney Harbour. Theirs was not a day of celebration but a day of remembrance, on which all Aborigines commemorated their ancestors and reminded non-Aboriginal Australians that their achievements had come at a cost of massive suffering.

On 26 January, 1988, the two tribes of

▲ *The centenary celebration marches past the centenary demonstration.*

▲ *The Aboriginal demonstration on Australia Day ends on La Perouse beach, where white explorers first landed 200 years before.*

Australia – the Aborigines and the non-Aborigines – came face to face with one another. Their two *Corroborees* became a single event. Although the non-Aborigines had set out to celebrate the achievements of their pioneers, they finished the day thinking more and more about the Aborigines. Something very important happened on Australia Day: a new beginning was made. It was the start of a period in which the Aborigines are being recognized as important parts of Australian society.

At the other end of the globe a smaller but no less important event happened. Aboriginal elder Burnum Burnum, from the Aboriginal peoples of Eastern Australia, planted an Aboriginal flag at Dover and claimed the whole of the United Kingdom on behalf of the Aboriginal peoples of Australia. The protest, of course, was symbolic.

It would be ridiculous to think that real annexation of Britain by the Aborigines was possible. Just as ridiculous as it was for the British in 1788 to arrive in a land 20,000 km away and with the simple act of planting a flag claim it on behalf of their king.

The picture of the Aborigines of Australia is of a mixture of dismay and hope. On the one hand Aboriginal culture is in crisis. Many Aboriginal communities are characterized by alcoholism, drug taking, premature deaths and violence. But on the other hand, some Aborigines are now claiming better education and housing, and insisting on being treated equally. For them the future is an exciting place where Aborigines and non-Aborigines stand as equals; where Aboriginal culture is thought to be important to all Australians.

Glossary

Aborigine   The first occupants of any land. Often used more specifically to mean the 500 or so tribal groups of pre-colonization Australia. The words *Nyoongar* and *Koori* are now also being used to describe them.

Apartheid   A system of government in South Africa that made people live in certain places according to the colour of their skin. White people got all the best places to live.

Cattle barons   Owners of large areas of land on which huge herds of cattle are raised.

Contemporary   Modern, present-day.

Corroborree   An Aboriginal celebration, often held at night, including music and dancing.

Depression   The name of a time in the early 1930s when very few people had jobs or enough money to live on.

Dreamtime   An English term used by Aborigines to refer to the time of creation.

Emu   Large birds that live in Australia. They cannot fly, but run quickly.

Full-blood   An English term for Aborigines whose families have never had children with white people and who have not adopted many non-Aborigine ways.

Guerilla war   A war in which one side tries to stay hidden from the other, attacking in unexpected places and disappearing before they are caught.

Illiterate   Unable to read.

Infant mortality   The number of babies in every thousand born that die. Infant mortality is used to measure how good health care is in particular groups of people.

Joy-riding   Driving very fast in a stolen car.

Marsupial   Mammals whose young are born and then continue to develop in a 'pouch'.

Mission   Places at which representatives of one of the Christian religions live. They try to make the local people join their religion.

Nomadic   Constantly moving, usually in search of food to eat and pasture for animals.

Ochre   Orange or yellowish-orange.

Outback   The remote, wild country away from the settled areas of Australia.

Polluted   Made unclean or not pure.

Poverty   Lack of enough food, shelter or clothing.

Prejudice   An idea of what someone or something will be like before you have met or seen them. For example, if you thought all Aborigines were stupid but had never met one, you would be prejudiced against Aborigines.

Racist   Prejudiced against someone because of their race.

Reserve   An area of land set aside for the use of a particular group of Aborigines.

Rural   In the countryside; away from the towns and cities.

Segregation   Keeping things apart. Most often used to describe the policy of racial segregation; making people with different-coloured skins live in different areas. See apartheid.

Suburb   An area in which people live outside the centre of a city.

Uluru   The enormous rock in the desert at the centre of Australia, which has great spiritual significance for the Aborigines. Also called Ayers Rock.

Urban   Part of the city.

Woomera   An implement used to throw a spear.

Further reading

For younger readers:
The Gaia Atlas of First Peoples Julian Berger (Gaia Books, 1990)
Australian Aborigines, Peoples of the World series, Anne Smith (Wayland, 1989). Peoples of the World is a series aimed at younger readers.
Survival International Junior Action Pack (Survival International, 1991)

For older readers:
Gularbulu Paddy Roe (Fremantle Arts Centre Press, 1983)
My Place Sally Morgan (Fremantle Arts Centre Press, 1987)
The Songlines Bruce Chatwin (Picador, 1988)
Joe Nangan's Dreaming Joe Nangan (Nelson Australia, 1976)

Further information

Australian High Commissions and Embassies in your own country are a good first stop in your search for more information. You could also try the following:

Australia

The Aboriginal Centre
Old Clontarf Boys Home
Manning Road
Waterford 6152

Australian Institute of Aboriginal Studies
PO Box 553
Canberra 2601

Redfern Legal Centre
Everleigh Street
Redfern 2016

Canada

Indigenous Survival International
47 Clarence Street
Suite 300
Ottawa
Ontario K1N 9K1

UK

Mr James Hunt AO
Australian Book Shop
10 Woburn Walk
London WC1

Minority Rights Group
379 Brixton Road
London SW9 7DE

USA

Survival International
2121 Decataur Place NW
Washington DC 20008

Index

Numbers in **bold** refer to pictures as well as text.